Settle Conflicts
Right Now!

Jan L. Osier ■ Harold P. Fox

Settle Conflicts
Right Now!

A Step-by-Step Guide for K-6 Classrooms

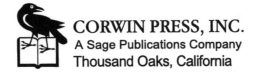
CORWIN PRESS, INC.
A Sage Publications Company
Thousand Oaks, California

Copyright © 2001 by Corwin Press, Inc.

For information:

Corwin Press, Inc.
A Sage Publications Company
2455 Teller Road
Thousand Oaks, California 91320
E-mail: order@corwinpress.com

Sage Publications Ltd.
6 Bonhill Street
London EC2A 4PU
United Kingdom

Sage Publications India Pvt. Ltd.
M-32 Market
Greater Kailash I
New Delhi 110 048 India

Printed in the United States of America

Library of Congress Cataloging-in-Publication Data

Osier, Jan L.
   Settle conflicts right now!: A step-by-step guide for K-6 classrooms / by Jan L. Osier and Harold P. Fox.
       p.   cm.
     ISBN 0-7619-7760-0 (c: alk. paper)
     ISBN 0-7619-7761-9 (p: alk. paper)
     1. Conflict management—Study and teaching (Elementary)—Activity programs. 2. School violence—Prevention.
   I. Fox, Harold P.   II. Title.
   LB3013.3.O85 2000
   372.1102'4-dc21   00-011237

This book is printed on acid-free paper.

01   02   03   04   05   06   10   9   8   7   6   5   4   3   2   1

Corwin Editorial Assistant:	Julia Parnell
Production Editor:	Nevair Kabakian
Editorial Assistant:	Cindy Bear
Typesetter/Designer:	D&G Limited, LLC
Cover Designer:	Michael Dubowe

Contents

Preface

This book was written primarily for elementary school teachers to provide you with the tools needed to help your students resolve their own conflicts, regardless of their age, sex, or ethnicity. Our experience underscores the fact that children *can* attain the skills needed to handle basic conflicts found in a variety of social situations. Basic, everyday life conflicts *can* be resolved without resorting to verbal or physical aggression.

Settle Conflicts Right Now! was designed specifically for use in classrooms and schools, although the principles can be applied in a variety of social settings, including homes. This conflict resolution program teaches a technique individuals can apply to resolve conflicts before, during, or after they occur. Through the use of simple cognitive skills, individuals can focus on resolution so the problem will not recur.

Written for use by educators, students, administrators, counselors, and parents, this book provides a unique method of conflict resolution that can be applied by both younger and older children. Unlike other conflict resolution programs that employ the use of mediators, this program instead teaches a method of conflict resolution that enables individuals to seek a solution to their problem without the intervention of others. In addition, our program was designed for the teacher to make conflict resolution easy, practical, fast, and effective in the classroom. Our program facilitates a solution between the parties involved and provides written documentation of that solution for parents, administrators, and teachers.

The conflict resolution process described in this book can be introduced to a class in as few as three to four short lessons (of approximately 30 minutes each). It can be practiced using real-life incidents or made-up ones. The actual time it takes to settle a conflict could be a matter of minutes, but typically it will take 15 to 45 minutes. The amount of time needed depends on how well you are able to acquire and use the techniques described. Full mastery of our conflict resolution process will result in your being able to produce quicker results in a shorter time. Once you have become familiar with this process, you will find that you are in total control. You will not fear conflict, because you will have a method to apply uniformly when resolving conflict situations. Additionally, our process is designed to prevent you from being caught in the middle of other peoples' conflicts. You will never again have to endure the pain of being judge or jury or suffer from the agony of wondering if you made the right decision while resolving someone else's problem. You do not have to render decisions or justice. Instead, you learn to act as a facilitator who allows the people involved to solve their own conflict.

Please read the entire book before you begin using *Settle Conflicts Right Now!* We encourage you to practice our process until you feel comfortable with it. The chapters are designed to provide you with the tools necessary for successful conflict resolution both in the home and a school setting. Chapters 1 and 2 explain the process and how it works. Chapter 3 shows you how to use this process in a classroom situation. Chapter 4 illustrates how easy it is to set up basic conflict resolution centers that can be used in a variety of locations within a school. Chapters 5 and 6 tell how to use this process in a counseling situation and at home. Resource A gives samples of how the technique works, and Resource B answers questions that are commonly asked about our program.

Settle Conflicts Right Now! uses writing or drawing as an aid to clarify issues and produce solutions. Reproducible worksheets and posters outlining the steps to follow are provided for use by anyone who is able to write or draw. Older children use writing to resolve conflict, and younger children or children with limited verbal ability use drawing. Whether drawing or writing, the motor response produces a reduction in anger and promotes truthfulness and a peaceful resolution.

Anyone can learn how to resolve basic conflicts using the technique described in this book. This approach does not cause individuals to lose face or worry that someone else is getting more "justice" than they are. This approach will enable all using it to employ the social skill of empathy. They will realize that the other person—regardless of sex, age, or race —feels pain just as they do. This internalized understanding or awareness that others "feel pain like I do" is what resolves conflicts successfully.

Today, over 3,000 schools in the United States are teaching conflict resolution skills as a part of their daily curriculum, thus creating adults that have the skills needed to handle conflict in a peaceful manner. We hope that through the use of conflict resolution, schools and communities will enjoy freedom from violence and aggression. We know that *Settle Conflicts Right Now!* will give you a successful way to create peace and harmony in your life and the lives of the people around you. Thank you for helping to create peace by teaching the strategies of peaceful conflict resolution!

Acknowledgments

Our program could not have been created without the support and guidance from friends, colleagues, and family. We wish to thank the following people for helping us to bring our project to its final form: Martin J. Osier, Mary Kathleen Osier, Jennifer M. Osier, Paul Fox, Stephanie Fox, Christopher Fox, Sandra J. Wrightson, Theresa F. M. Jones, Frankie Nielsen, Patricia Preston, Melba Brown, Letch Connell, Holly Beecroft, Martin Kinney, Walter Wilhoit, Beverly Erdmann, and Jan Colvin. We would also like to acknowledge the faculty and administration at Bamberg American High School, Wuerzburg Middle School, and Vilseck Elementary School for their support and willingness to try a new method of conflict resolution. Finally, this program would not exist without our wonderful students, who work diligently every day to resolve conflict peacefully. Thank you!

The contributions of the following reviewers are gratefully acknowledged:

- Linda Carey, Assistant Professor, Special Education
  Center for Excellence in Education,
  Northern Arizona University
  Flagstaff, AZ

- Judith Emmett, Professor of Counseling
  Counseling and School Psychology Department,
  University of Wisconsin-River Falls
  River Falls, WI

- Kevin A. Fall, Assistant Professor
  Department of Education and Counseling,
  Loyola University New Orleans
  New Orleans, LA

- Betty Hubschman, Assistant Professor
  School of Education,
  Barry University
  Miami, FL

- Joanne D. Newcombe, Professor of Educational Leadership
  School of Education and Allied Studies,
  Bridgewater State College
  Bridgewater, MA

Jan L. Osier
Bamberg, Germany

Harold P. Fox
Wuerzburg, Germany

About the Authors

Jan L. Osier works for the Department of Defense Schools (DODDS) in Bamberg, Germany, as a learning impaired teacher for Grades 7 through 12. She has also worked extensively with special education learning disabled students in Grades K through 12 in Montana. As a special educator, she has had the opportunity to work with parents and teachers as a resource consultant on behavioral issues and learning impairments. Her past experience in working with children with behavior disorders and children of prison inmates has given her valuable insight into the need for teaching children nonviolent conflict resolution skills. She is coauthor of *I Can Solve My Own Problems,* published in 1993, and has won numerous awards for her teaching skills, including the Wuerzburg District Teacher of the Year award. She currently sits as a member of the DODDS National Advisory Panel for Children with Disabilities in Washington, D.C. She graduated with honors from Eastern Montana College in Billings, Montana, with a bachelor of science degree in special education with an emphasis on behavior disorders and has a master of education degree in curriculum and instruction from National-Louis University in Chicago, Illinois. She enjoys reading, music, writing, and travel and lives with her husband, Marty, and youngest child, Katie, in Bamberg, Germany.

Harold P. Fox is a middle school counselor for the Department of Defense Schools (DODDS) in Wuerzburg, Germany. He has taught in the Los Angeles Unified School District and East High School in Anchorage, Alaska, and has had extensive experience working as a counselor and teacher in all grade levels from kindergarten to college. As a counselor and educator, he has focused on giving children of all ages a better way of resolving conflict. His own philosophy of conflict resolution has been heavily influenced by the Yoruba approach to conflict resolution. He is coauthor of *I Can Solve My Own Problems,* published in 1993. He graduated summa cum laude from the University of California, Berkeley with a bachelor of arts degree in social science and has a master of science degree in counseling from California State University, at Los Angeles. His hobbies are music, reading, and travel. He enjoys playing blues piano and has worked as a professional musician with his own Brown Bag Blues Band. He has two children.

Dedication

To all the students at Bindlach Elementary School for showing us a "better way" to resolve conflict!

In loving memory of
Betty Pharaoh

Solving Problems
With Conflict Resolution

Whether you are a teacher, manager, parent, counselor, or a citizen in today's society, you may have noticed that there is a distressing lack of peaceful conflict resolution skills among people today. Many people don't understand compromise, give and take, tolerance, and patience. What this kind of an attitude can do in a school or community is disturbing. It creates senseless violence and overreaction to everyday conflict. By learning a concrete method of resolving conflict, children and adults are better prepared to face the difficulties involved in communicating with other individuals. By learning alternate ways to communicate their needs, adults and children can better resolve their conflicts and do not need the help of others to solve their problems peacefully. Increased self-esteem, understanding the needs of others, and expressing feelings in a positive way are the natural by-products of learning to resolve conflict in a peaceful manner. The idea behind *Settle Conflicts Right Now!* is a simple one. It is based on the idea that to create peace, we must teach the attitude and skill necessary to bring about peace. In our society today, we find two basic approaches to conflict resolution. The first is the approach most often taken by children and adults. We call this the "visceral route." The visceral route isn't effective and doesn't result in a satisfactory resolution for all parties involved in the conflict. In comparison, the "processing route" demonstrated by *Settle Conflicts Right Now!* is a better way of resolving conflict. It taps into peoples' emotional intelligence and gives them a format they can use that results in a lasting solution. The chart that follows outlines the two approaches and their differences.

Children and adults learn that empathy and compromise are often the key to resolving conflict. They also learn that resolution is possible if the parties involved want to end the pain of conflict. We often hear from teachers, adults, and children that as they use the program, they begin to apply it only when it is really needed and less and less with small conflicts. After children and adults become experts at using the process, they internalize the steps needed to the point where they can "think it, say it, and talk it out." *Settle Conflicts Right Now!* becomes an automatic response to conflict situations resulting in fewer conflicts and lasting resolutions.

Most conflicts are not resolved unless all parties involved get *their* needs met in some way. This means that the people in conflict must share what they think needs to be done to resolve the conflict. This is often hard

---

VIEWPOINT

Visceral Route	Processing Route
• You have an instinctual and emotional response to conflict.	• You have a thoughtful and empathetic response to conflict.
• You are put in a cycle of perpetual pain!	• You are put in a process to share your pain.
• The situation leads to dehumanizing acts of verbal abuse and physical aggression.	• Information is shared and transferred.
• You end up "trading pain to end pain."	• You discover that the other person hurts and experiences pain like you do.
• Pain escalates.	• You understand each other's pain.
• Your body and mind can't handle it.	• The healing process starts.
• Last vain effort to trade pain fails.	• You share and trade information.
• Intervention by others doesn't last long.	• You are willing to give and understand each other.
• You decide to get revenge.	• It works! You're relieved of the pain.
• You descend emotionally to the level of an animal.	• You get what you need and give others what they need.
• It fails!	• You stay human and feel understood.
• You don't know what you did or why you did it.	• The PAIN ends!
• You stay in PAIN!	

for adults and children to understand, particularly if they feel that they are the only victim in the conflict. Human nature seeks punishment for the aggressor, and often the victim feels that the person who caused the conflict has no right to have their needs met. Conflicts are not that simple, and usually both parties are involved to varying degrees. For conflict to end, blame has to be taken out of the equation. By sharing needs and solutions, rather than blame, a final resolution that is lasting can be reached.

The Step-by-Step Program:
An Overview

The ability to resolve conflict is an inherent human skill necessary for survival. This program uses the basic cognitive skills of sharing, reading, writing, listening, speaking, and thinking. These skills are an integral part of all students' academic learning and a part of most adults' everyday lives.

The purpose of this chapter is to

- Identify who can effectively use this program.
- Identify appropriate settings.
- Provide a brief overview of how this program is used.

Who Can Effectively Use This Program?

This program can be used by students, educators, parents, administrators, counselors, and any other person who is in a position to learn or teach basic conflict resolution skills. It was specifically written for teachers, who more than most people, spend enormous amounts of time resolving conflict. The program reverses that trend by allowing teachers time to teach while giving students a way of handling their own problems with little teacher intervention.

Where Should You Use This Program?

Conflicts occur naturally in all settings. Home, school, work—everywhere you have people working with one another, you have the potential for conflict. Some conflicts are small and can be resolved quite easily. Other conflicts are large and complex. *All* conflicts can be resolved, given time and the appropriate tools for resolution. This program provides the basic tools needed to resolve conflicts in a variety of settings, particularly schools. If the parties involved have time and the availability of paper and pencil, then the tools are in place for resolving conflict.

In the classroom setting, a conflict resolution center can be established as a place for children to go to resolve their conflicts with each other. Students use the step-by-step process to help them organize their thoughts and share their feelings. Ground rules are established to avoid blame, fault-finding, condemnation, or judgment and focus totally on resolution. For other individuals, a traveling conflict center can be used, or they can simply use the basic steps of the process as it is needed.

This method can be expanded for use in a variety of settings. Because the program is a basic problem-solving program, it can be used effectively with both hypothetical and real-life situations. Many teachers have found that it is a useful tool in science, literature, and history to analyze characters, evaluate decisions, and solve problems. Parents can use it at home with their children and with each other, spouse to spouse. Adults can use it in the workplace, with children, or as individuals trying to resolve a personal problem that doesn't necessarily involve others.

How Do You Use This Program?

The following pages contain the steps needed to help individuals and groups solve their own problems. Like any good program, it takes practice to make it work. We suggest that you practice using the teaching activities before trying it with individuals or groups having a real conflict.

The program follows the same process regardless of what age level you are working with. Younger children draw and explain, older children write and read to facilitate a resolution to their problem. The basic steps to the whole program are outlined. The fine details for implementing these steps are included in the remaining chapters of this book.

The Basic Process

In this process of conflict resolution, students

- Learn to use the program.
- Use the program themselves in a conflict center.
- Write or draw why they are upset.
- Exchange papers and learn why the other person is upset.
- Write or draw what they think needs to be done to help end the conflict.
- Exchange papers and share their solutions.
- Mark or initial, in color, on the other person's paper what they agree to do to help end the conflict.

In a school setting, the Color Code of Honor (the colored check marks or initials) becomes the contract between each person that indicates what he or she will do to end the conflict.

Resolving Conflict in the Classroom

It is important to note that many children disagree with each other and at times resolve conflict in ineffectual ways. They fight with their peers, their siblings, their teachers, and their parents. This system will help them identify their problem, state their role in the problem, state what they think needs to be done to resolve the problem, and establish a compromise that will ensure the conflict does not recur. This program will empower children to feel better about what may be happening to them and to sort out their responsibilities concerning the problem. We have found that children are willing to compromise if they feel that their side of the problem has been heard and if others involved are willing to compromise, too. It is important that no blame or judgment be placed on the actions of any person involved in the problem. The goal must always be to focus on resolving the conflict so that it won't recur.

This chapter is divided into four sections. Each section outlines the steps needed to introduce the program and put it in place for children to use at different ages.

- Section 3-1. General Instruction for Classroom Use
- Section 3-2. Plans and Materials for Grades K-2

- Section 3-3. Plans and Materials for Grades 3-6
- Section 3-4. Documenting Student Conflict and a Letter for Parents

3-1. General Instructions for Classroom Use

The following flowchart outlines the preparation needed to introduce and use this program in the classroom. This preparation is needed for all grade levels for students to clearly understand how to use the program and for them to be able to use the program independently in Grades 3-12.

Before actually using the program to solve real conflicts, you must establish with the students ground rules for resolving conflict. Below is a sample list of guidelines that you might consider for your classroom. Feel free

PREPARATIONS FOR USING THE PROGRAM

TEACHER PREPARATION

- Read lesson plans carefully.
- Understand the steps on the teaching posters for your grade level.
- Plan for sessions needed to introduce the procedure to students.
- Note: This makes a good health, reading, or writing lesson.

STUDENT PREPARATION

- Make sure each student has a pencil, markers, or crayons.
- Give each student a copy of the resolution sheets that match their grade level.
- Give each student a copy of the activity card needed.

CLASSROOM PREPARATION

- Read chapter four to learn how to make a Conflict Resolution Center. Make sure it is ready to use.
- Copy resolution worksheets for class.
- Have extra copies of the teaching posters for students.

PARENT PREPARATION

- Send home parent letter telling parents about the Conflict Resolution Center in your classroom.
- Prepare parents for any documentation you might give them regarding their child and future conflicts. i.e. copies of the resolution sheets or documentation sheets for your classroom.

to make your own guidelines together with your students. One guideline to establish is to determine when you will allow students to use the classroom conflict resolution center described in the next chapter.

Ground Rules for Conflict Resolution

1. No yelling or talking out of turn
2. Each person's privacy and confidentiality will be respected
3. People may use the center at any time during the day
4. Each person may use words he or she wishes that are helpful in explaining the problem, but words that are hurtful are not allowed
5. If any person is disruptive, that person may be asked to leave until he or she is ready to begin to solve the conflict
6. If any person isn't ready to resolve the problem, then normal discipline procedures will be followed

---

Activity Cards

Activity cards are hypothetical situations that portray very real situations that children might find themselves in today. The following pages explain how to use activity cards in the classroom and provide sample activity cards to use in teaching the Settle Conflicts Right Now! technique to children. By selecting an appropriate situation, you will be able to provide children with a practice activity that matches conflicts occurring in their lives right now. The scenarios written on each card cover a wide range of situations.

Another source for activity cards can be found in comic strips and in history. Many comic strips have humorous conflicts that students and adults can identify with. It's fun to use comic strips involving two characters. By using the process to resolve the characters' conflict themselves, students can then compare their resolutions with the resolution provided by the author of the comic strip. History is another great source for evaluating hypothetical conflict situations between countries and people and then comparing the class resolution with the real-life resolution. The chance to rewrite history can be fun for students.

In the classroom, you might want to take common conflict situations that are occurring in your school or classroom and put them in a hypothetical setting with hypothetical characters. After resolving the hypothetical situation, ask the class if this situation has ever occurred in their lives.

They should recognize similarities and be able to discuss differences in outcomes between the hypothetical situation and the real-life situation. This kind of discussion can give students ways of handling conflict situations when they occur in the future.

How to Use Activity Cards in the Classroom

Teachers should select one of the activity cards that is appropriate to their classroom and then use the lesson plans provided to introduce the process. After the procedure is introduced, plan to allow students time to practice. The following pages contain activity cards and sample scenarios for writing your own cards for practice.

Activity Card 1

Mariah is riding the bus to school. Kateesha, another girl on the bus, is having a bad day, and she calls Mariah a bad name. Mariah is very upset and mad at Kateesha. When they get off the bus, they start yelling at each other and shoving each other until a teacher arrives and breaks up the fight. Both children are taken to the office for fighting, and both children are still mad at each other. What is the solution to their problem?

Activity Card 2

Sam has a great baseball card collection that he isn't supposed to bring to school. He decides to bring the cards to school anyway, and he puts them in his backpack so his parents won't notice. At school, he shows them to his friends, puts them back into his backpack, and leaves the backpack in the classroom when he goes out for recess. At recess, his friends Keith and Kenya tell him that James has stolen his baseball cards. He believes them, so he confronts James and says he wants the cards back. James is upset about being accused of taking the cards. He says he doesn't have the cards, but Keith and Kenya say that he has them and stole them from Sam. They continue arguing until they get back to the classroom. In the classroom, the cards are in the backpack, but Keith and Kenya still want Sam to beat up James. They say he took them and then put them back. James says he didn't do anything at all and that Keith and Kenya are liars. They argue so much that they are all sent to the office to get the problem straightened out. What is the solution to this problem?

Activity Card 3

Amy hears John call her a bad name in the hallway at school. She tells her teacher, and the teacher talks to John. John says he didn't call Amy a bad name. The teacher isn't sure if John called Amy a bad name, so she warns John about using bad language and sends him back to his desk. Amy is unhappy because she feels that John got away with calling her a name, so she tells her best friend, Charles, about the problem. He corners John at recess and is going to beat up John for calling Amy a bad name. What is the solution to this problem?

Scenarios for Writing Your Own Activity Cards

- **Friendship.** Trust is violated when one person tells a secret about another person.
- **Name Calling.** A child goes to Child A and says, "Guess what Child B is saying about you." Then this student goes to Child B and says, "Guess what Child A just said about you."
- **Stealing.** A person has something missing from his or her desk and blames another person without proof.
- **Taking Turns.** Two children want the same toy and can't find a way to take turns.
- **Refusing to Work.** A child is having a bad day and refuses to work or talk to the teacher or his or her parents.

An alternative way to use these cards in the classroom is to have students role-play the situation presented on the card. They use the process outlined previously to resolve the conflict while the rest of the class observes. Afterwards, the class can discuss how the process worked, why it worked, and if they would have done things differently. You can have two groups do the same role-play and discuss the similarities and differences in their solutions. Finally, you can present the role-plays to parents so they can see what your class is doing to learn conflict resolution.

3-2. Plans and Materials for Grades K-2

This section contains an overview, lesson plans, and resolution sheets or posters (or both) for the classroom. Young children who can't read, write, or have limited verbal ability can use this program effectively. Teachers working with second-grade students have the option of using this section to introduce the program or using Section 3-3. If students can write well enough to communicate their feelings and read well enough to comprehend what another student has written, then we suggest you use the materials in Section 3-3.

Begin by following the lesson plan to introduce the process to your students. After they are familiar with the process, then you need to decide if they will use the conflict resolution center alone, without supervision, or if you want to be the facilitator. You might try it both ways and see which works best for your students. Keep in mind the severity of the conflict and the maturity of your students, which may require your facilitation of a resolution. Students gain independence at a variety of ages, so some will be able to follow this process very easily by themselves, and others will need guidance at this young age.

The steps below give a brief overview of how the program works when it is first taught and how the program functions when students use it in a real-life situation.

Overview of Steps

Teaching Situation   Students will be asked to listen to a story that has at least two characters involved in a conflict. They must identify and draw a picture of each character's problem as they understand it. They then must draw a picture of a solution that they think will end the conflict. The solution should be what each character thinks should happen so everyone feels happy again. The different solutions are reviewed by the students. Each solution that is agreed upon is marked with a colored marker.

Real-Life Conflict Situation   Each person in conflict must draw a picture of the problem using Resolution Sheet 1: Draw the Problem. They should each tell the other person about their picture. Then they must draw a picture of what they would like to see happen so that the problem will be solved using Resolution Sheet 2: Draw the Solution. They should again tell the other person about their picture. They should exchange papers and select a colored marker. If they agree to what is in the picture, then they should make a mark of some kind next to all they agree to do. The picture is given back to the owner. All items in each picture that have a mark next to them are called the Color Code of Honor. This is the final solution to the problem.

Lesson Plan: Grades K-2

The following lesson plan is designed to introduce conflict resolution to young children and children who have difficulty reading and writing. This lesson plan can be adapted, combined, or revised to meet your own individual needs. This is a sample lesson plan using Activity Card 1 found in Section 3-1. You can use this card to introduce students to the program.

Like any program, please read each step before you implement it so you know exactly what to do and when to do it.

Objective   To introduce students to the procedure for resolving conflicts using drawing.

Time   Three 15- to 30-minute lessons. Each lesson is clearly written but does not put words into your mouth to use with children. Present the material in a way that you are comfortable, but follow the sequence outlined for each lesson.

The Conflict   The conflict used is the story presented in Activity Card 1 from Section 3-1 or your own scenario. Whatever material you choose to use, you must make sure that there are two characters or groups of characters involved in a conflict with each other in the story.

Method of Instruction   Whole group.

Materials Needed

- Activity card
- Chart tablet or overhead projector
- Overlays of resolution sheets for overhead projector
- Copies of resolution sheets for each student
- Pencils, markers, and overhead projector pens

Lesson 1

1. Read Activity Card 1 to the class and discuss who the characters are and what happened in the story.
2. Give each student a copy of Resolution Sheet 1: Draw the Problem. Let the students pretend they are Mariah from the activity card. Have them draw a picture on the resolution sheet that shows Mariah's problem.
3. Walk around asking questions about the pictures. Label actions and characters on the worksheets as you have time.
4. Ask students to share and tell about their pictures. Write down Mariah's problem on the chart tablet. Label the chart "The Problem." Remind the students that they are thinking about and telling all the problems they think Mariah had in the story.
5. Collect all the pictures to display in the room. The next lesson should be the next day.

Lesson 2

1. Read the story again if necessary. Read the problems identified on the chart from Lesson 2.

2. Hand out a new Resolution Sheet 1. Tell the students to pretend they are Kateesha, the second character on Activity Card 1. Have them draw a picture on their worksheet that shows the problem Kateesha had in the story.

3. Walk around and ask questions for clarification. Label actions and characters on the resolution sheet.

4. Ask for students to share and tell about their pictures. Write the problems identified for Kateesha on a new chart.

5. Collect all the worksheets and display them in the room for the next lesson. The next lesson should be the next day.

Lesson 3

1. Review the story and charts from the previous lessons.

2. Hand out Resolution Sheet 2: Draw the Solution. Tell the students that they need to draw a picture that shows what could be done to make all the characters in the story happy.

3. After everyone is finished, then ask students to share their solutions. Write them on the chart and display all three charts in the room. Take a colored marker and have the class vote on each solution. Mark all the actions on the chart that the whole class agrees will solve the problem in the story. These colored marks are called the Color Code of Honor. Explain to the class that the Color Code of Honor shows all the solutions that everyone agrees will solve the problem. If they were in a conflict with another person, these colored marks would show what they agree to do to solve the problem. Explain that the colored marks are a promise that you give to the other person to show what you will do to solve the problem.

4. Give each student a conflict resolution certificate (found in Chapter 4) for successfully solving the problem that was presented.

5. Have each student staple the worksheets into a booklet with a blank page for the cover. Let them design a cover for their conflict resolution booklet.

You might want to consider repeating these lessons to make sure students understand and can use the process successfully. Use any story that has at least two characters involved in a conflict.

Resolution Sheets and Teaching Posters

The resolution sheets on the following pages can be used as posters for your classroom conflict resolution center. Rather than having separate posters, it is less confusing for young children to see and follow posters that are exactly the same as the resolution sheets they will use to resolve their problem. You can add any symbols or visual cues you feel necessary to help students use the resolution sheets independently in the classroom conflict resolution center.

After students have learned how to use the resolution sheets, we suggest that they be photocopied back to back so that the children have only one sheet of paper to use. They start with Resolution Sheet 1 and turn it over to complete Resolution Sheet 2. Another way to simplify the use of the resolution sheets is to staple them into a booklet using the cover sheet found in Chapter 4. This makes a booklet that can be sent home with the student when they are done.

DRAW THE PROBLEM!

NAME: _____

RESOLUTION SHEET 1

DRAW THE SOLUTION!

RESOLUTION
SHEET
2

NAME: _____

3-3. Plans and Materials for Grades 3-6

Students in these grades usually are able to read, write, and follow instructions independently. They enjoy and look forward to resolving conflicts on their own. A conflict resolution center in the classroom will empower them to use their skills to solve problems on their own. Anger is often defused by writing, because writing takes away judgment, threat, and anger. Students will find it easier to write their needs rather than say them. In addition, students quite often find it hard to lie on paper. This section contains the lesson plans, resolution sheets, and classroom posters you need for using this program with independent readers and writers.

The steps below give a brief overview of how the program works when it is first taught and how it functions when students use it in a real-life situation.

Overview of Steps

Teaching Situation   Students will be asked to identify characters presented in a hypothetical situation and to recognize the conflict in the situation. They will be asked to identify the problem presented from both characters' points of view. They will then identify possible solutions to the problem. The solutions are voted on and marked with a colored marker to indicate the final solutions.

Real-Life Conflict Situation   Each person in conflict will be asked to go to the classroom conflict resolution center. They must follow the teaching posters posted at the center. They must use Resolution Sheet 1: What's the Problem to write down their problems with each other. They should exchange papers and each read aloud what the other person has written. On Resolution Sheet 2: What I Need to Solve This Problem, they again exchange papers and read aloud what the other person has written. At this point, each person should take a colored marker and check off the statements on Resolution Sheet 2 that they will agree to do. They should give the paper back to the other person. This paper becomes the Color Code of Honor that lists the agreed-upon solutions.

Lesson Plan: Grades 3-6

The following lesson plan is designed to foster independent conflict resolution skills in students who are able to read and write. This lesson plan can be adapted, combined, or revised to meet your individual needs. The lesson plans with the activity cards found in Section 3-1 can be used to introduce the process to students.

Like any program, read each step before you use this program, so that you know exactly what to do and when to do it.

Objective   To teach the program and all the steps involved for using it to solve a conflict.

Time   Four 30- to 45-minute lessons.

The Conflict   An activity card from Section 3-1 or your own scenario. Whatever material you choose to use, you must make sure that there are two characters involved in a conflict with each other in the story.

Method of Instruction   Whole group or whole class instruction for Lessons 1, 2, and 3. For Lesson 4, students are put into pairs.

Materials Needed

- Activity card
- Chart tablet or overhead projector
- Overlays of resolution sheets for overhead projector
- Copies of resolution sheets for each student
- Pencils, markers, and overhead projector pens

Lesson 1

1. Talk about the goal for this class. The goal is to help students learn a method to solve fighting, arguments, and conflict with each other. Explain that for students to learn this method, it will take four lessons to do it.

2. Hand out a copy of the activity card you have selected to each student.

3. Using the overhead projector or a chart tablet (previously prepared), display the card and read it to the students.

4. Have students identify each of the characters involved in the story on the activity card. List them on the overhead or chart as Character A, B, and so on.

5. Using a chart or overlay of Resolution Sheet 1: What's the Problem, have the students explain why Character A is upset. Write down their answers, in list form, on the chart or overlay.

6. Repeat Step 5 for Character B and so on.

7. Review the lists for all characters and add to them if necessary.

Lesson 2

1. Review the lists for Resolution Sheet 1 from Lesson 1.

2. Hand out the activity card used in Lesson 1 to each student.

3. Using a chart or overlay of Resolution Sheet 2: What I Need to Solve This Problem, have the students identify what Character A needs in order for him or her to feel happy again. Write down the students' answers in list form on the chart or overlay.

4. Repeat Step 3 for each character.

5. Review the lists for both characters and add to them if necessary to clarify meaning.

6. Tell the students that possible solutions have now been identified. Review Resolution Sheet 2 for each character. Use a colored marker to check off those solutions the class feels are the best.

7. The colored check marks on Resolution Sheet 2 are called the Color Code of Honor. These marks identify the solutions to the problem.

Lesson 3

1. Review all the steps it took to solve a conflict with the activity card used in Lessons 1 and 2.

2. If you are using a comic strip as an activity card, show the whole comic strip at this time so your students can see how the author resolved the issue.

3. Introduce the classroom conflict resolution center that you set up in your classroom at this time.

4. Show the students where everything is located in the center. Introduce the teaching posters that show how the process is done step by step. They can follow these posters in sequence if they forget what they need to do while they are at the center.

5. If time allows, pair up the students and give each individual a set of resolution sheets, an activity card, and a set of posters to follow. Have them work in pairs to resolve the conflict presented on the activity card. They must remember to resolve the conflict by pretending to be one of the characters on the activity card.

6. Stop students in a logical place and continue the pair lesson in Lesson 4.

Lesson 4

1. Continue the activity from Lesson 3.

2. After everyone has completed their card, ask for volunteers to tell about their problem and their solutions.

3. Again review how to use the resolution center. Go over the ground rules for your classroom and establish when students can and cannot use the center.

4. Have students write down what they think of the program and whether or not they are willing to use the resolution center. This information is valuable data to judge who may need more guidance when they first begin to use the center in your classroom.

Other Ways to Practice This Technique

- Use a story the students are currently reading that contains a problem involving two or more characters. Use Resolution Sheets 1 and 2 to analyze the problem and develop a solution. Remember to look back at the story to compare the author's solution with the students' solution.

- Use a character or conflict from history to analyze by using the resolution sheets. Compare the real solution with the students' solution.

- Put cards with characters' names and brief histories into a hat and have students draw out two characters. Let students, either individually or in groups, create a conflict to go with the characters and use the resolution sheets to outline their story. The students can then summarize the story by writing an activity card from the resolution sheets.

- Have students cut out comic strips or news articles from newspapers and magazines that show a conflict between characters. Use the resolution sheets to analyze the conflict and write a solution. Send the solution and worksheets to the author of the comic strip as a letter-writing activity as well as a problem-solving activity.

Resolution Sheets

The resolution sheets that follow are used by students to record their feelings about the conflict and what they would like to see happen in order for the conflict to end. They can be photocopied back to back so that students have one sheet, or they can be stapled together to make a booklet with a cover sheet that indicates your school name or classroom. A sample cover sheet can be found in Chapter 4. Copies of these single sheets or booklets need to be available in your classroom conflict resolution center.

It is important to make sure that you have clarified with students what you want them to do with their completed resolution sheets. The students usually want to keep copies of their hard work. You might make a photocopy of their work for your files and for parents.

WHAT'S THE PROBLEM?

Directions: In the space below, describe what was said or done to you that you did not like!

Tell how you felt when this experience happened to you. Tell what you did!

NAME _____

RESOLUTION SHEET 1

WHAT I NEED TO SOLVE THIS PROBLEM!

Directions: You have been hurt! You want something to happen that will help you feel better. Clearly describe what you think should happen to solve this problem!

NAME_____

_____

_____

_____

_____

_____

_____

_____

_____

_____

_____

_____

_____

_____

_____

_____

RESOLUTION SHEET 2

Classroom Posters

The following classroom posters can be used with the lesson plan and can be displayed in the conflict resolution center in your classroom. These posters outline the steps students follow to use this conflict resolution technique. To explain the process to parents, you might send a copy of these posters home, along with the parent letter (see Section 3-4), explaining the program.

STEP 1

If you are having a conflict with another person, you need to do the following:

1. Each of you get a copy of Resolution Sheet 1: What's The Problem?

2. Write your name on your paper. Give your paper to the other person to read.

CLASSROOM POSTER 1

STEP 2

After you have exchanged papers, you need to do the following:

1. Read the other person's paper to yourself.

2. Read the other person's paper aloud while the writer listens.

3. If you can't read what the other person wrote, or if you don't understand what was written, ask.

4. No arguing is allowed! You may use quiet voices only! Remember, you are here to solve your problem!

CLASSROOM POSTER 2

STEP 3

After you have finished STEP 2, you need to do the following:

1. Get your Resolution Sheet 1 back from the other person.

2. Follow the directions on Resolution Sheet 2: What I Need to Solve This Problem.

3. Write your name on your paper and trade papers with the other person.

4. Read the other person's paper silently and then read it aloud. If you don't understand what the person wrote, ask questions.

CLASSROOM POSTER 3

STEP 4

After you have finished STEP 3, you are ready to create a solution to your problem. Follow these steps:

1. Choose a colored marker from the conflict resolution center. You should still have the other person's paper in your hand.

2. Mark your initials on the other person's Resolution Sheet 2 next to the items that you agree to do to solve your problem.

3. Take turns telling each other what you marked on the paper so that the problem will end. When you talk to the other person, use their name.

4. Get your paper back. The colored initials on your paper are the COLOR CODE OF HONOR! This means that you have both agreed to these things in order to end your problem. This is a promise that you will do what is initialed on Resolution Sheet 2.

5. Congratulations! You have now solved your problem!

CLASSROOM POSTER 4

Osier & Fox, *Settle Conflicts Right Now! A Step-by-Step Guide for K–6 Classrooms.* Copyright © 2001 by Corwin Press, Inc.

3-4. Documenting Student Conflict and a Letter for Parents

The following is a list of methods for documenting conflict in a school setting. The purpose of documentation is to see if interventions are having a positive or negative impact on the student population and to isolate areas of conflict that may keep recurring. Included in this section are two sample documentation sheets for classroom use. Also included is a sample letter that can be sent home informing parents of the program and how you will use this program in your classroom.

Methods for Documenting Conflict Resolution at School

- In the conflict resolution center, have students sign in every time they go to the center to resolve a conflict. Have them check the general reason for using the center.

- Keep copies of all resolution sheets for each child who uses the conflict resolution center.

- Record the student's name and conflict if a child is sent to the office or use the school's discipline referral forms to maintain a record of students sent to the office or a counselor for intervention.

- Have the lunch monitors and playground aides use the same student log from the conflict resolution center to document incidents in their area.

- Use an observation sheet to have an observer record what he or she sees when a student is using the conflict resolution center. The observer can be a teacher, counselor, or administrator.

- Use a student roster for your classroom to make tally marks next to the student's name every time that student has to use the conflict resolution center. This will help you see how often the center is being used and who is using the center.

**Conflict Resolution Center
Sign-In Sheet**

Name	Fighting	Arguing Accusing Refusing	Stealing	Vandalism	Sent By Teacher	Asked To Go

Conflict Resolution Center
Observation Sheet

Observable Skills	Student 1 _____	Student 2 _____	Student 3 _____	Student 4 _____
Identified the Problem				
Listened to the Other Person				
Used a Helpful Voice				
Identified What He/ She Needed				
Helped to Solve the Problem				

Signature of Observer_____

Date of Observation_____

Observer is (circle one): teacher, counselor, administrator

Instructions to the observer: Write the names or initials of the people who are involved. Each time one of the people you are observing uses one of the identified skills, put a mark in the correct column.

Parent Letter

Date:_____

Dear Parents:

In our classroom this school year I am using an exciting new program called *Settle Conflicts Right Now!* This conflict resolution program teaches your child how to use their reading, thinking, writing, listening, and communication skills to solve everyday conflicts that occur at school and at home. The following is a list of components that are being used in our classroom:

- *whole group lessons to introduce the program*
- *a classroom conflict resolution center*
- *documentation of number and types of conflicts occurring in our class*
- *In the future, you may see copies of student resolution sheets come home with your child. This will show you that your child successfully solved his or her own problem. Please encourage your child to share the process he or she used and the resolution that was agreed upon regarding the conflict.*

If you have any questions about this program, please contact me. You are welcome to come into our classroom anytime to see the program in action.

Sincerely,

How to Make and Use a Conflict Resolution Center

Setting up a conflict resolution center in a classroom or at home is one way of helping those involved resolve their conflicts. After the program is introduced, a center can be set up to provide people with the worksheets and directions they need to use the center to solve real-life conflicts.

Setting Up a Classroom Conflict Resolution Center

In the classroom, each set of resolution sheets is placed in a labeled folder located at the center. A sample cover sheet is included at the end of this chapter. This cover sheet is attached to the conflict resolution sheets to make a booklet. The booklet is placed in the conflict resolution center and makes it easy for students to identify the resolution sheet packets they are to use in the center. We have also included certificates at the end of this chapter that can be given to students who have successfully completed the lessons and demonstrated proficiency in using the resolution center. Please note that the conflict resolution award certificate is for students using the drawing technique, and the other certificate is generic and can be used for all students. They are optional and can be given out when appropriate.

The implementation tips below are necessary for the center to be the most effective in your classroom.

Teacher Tips

- Students must be taught to use the program before the center is introduced and used.
- Teachers may initially have to supervise the center until students can use it effectively.
- Students must be given time to use the center either immediately after the conflict occurs or sometime during that day.
- As a follow-up, teachers must read what the students have written and give appropriate positive feedback. If possible, this should be done the same day that the conflict was resolved.
- Students who have to draw and dictate their program will need teacher or counselor assistance to facilitate the process.
- Decide which types of conflicts you will use with the center and which conflicts require disciplinary action or a referral to the counselor. The choice is yours; however, we suggest that conflicts involving weapons and physical injury be handled as a disciplinary action. To keep such situations from recurring, use this conflict process as a follow-up.

Student Tips

- Students may be sent to the center by their teacher
- Students must ask to go to the center before they go on their own
- Students must complete the resolution sheets and hand them in
- If a conflict can't be resolved, the students must see the teacher

The following are four different types of conflict resolution centers that can be used in any setting:

Center 1: Bulletin Board Center

Materials Needed:

- Multiple copies of resolution sheets to place in center
- Construction paper to make a pocket to hold resolution sheets
- A sign to identify the center
- A table under the bulletin board with chairs and space for students to write (clipboards on chairs can be used in place of the table)
- Pens and pencils in a container on the table
- Posters from Sections 3-2 or 3-3 to display on the bulletin board in sequence for students to follow

How to Use Center 1

This center is attached to a bulletin board. A separate small table is located under or near the board to hold materials that can't be attached to the board. Materials can be taken to other places in the room or worked on at the table.

Center 2: Folder on a Table

Materials Needed:

- A set of posters from Section 3-3 that shows how to use the program step by step (the posters can be mounted on tag board and opened like an accordion on top of the table or attached to the back of the table)

- Resolution sheets to insert into a folder that lays on top of the table
- A sign that stands on the table to identify the center
- Markers, pencils, and clipboards for writing

How to Use Center 2

This center is set up in a corner of the room and has a table for people to write on. The materials are set on the table and the posters are taped to the top of the table showing the steps to follow.

Center 3: Conflict Resolution Box

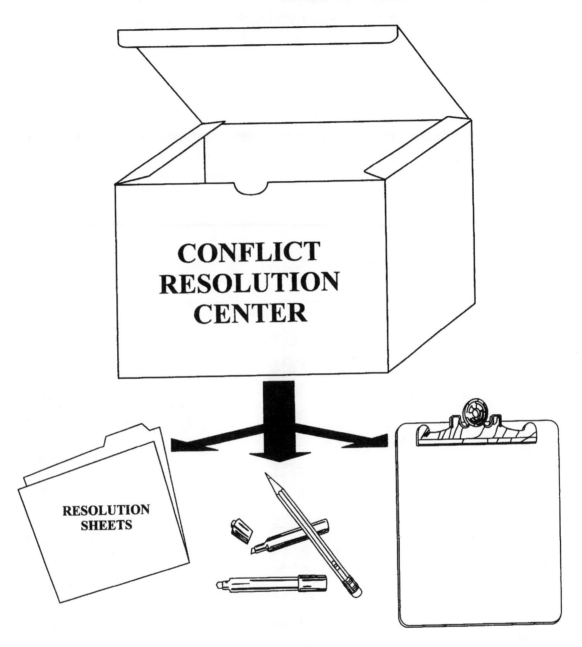

Materials Needed:

- A small box for all material
- Pencils, markers, and clipboards for writing
- Resolution sheets

- Posters stapled together in a booklet for students to follow
- A label for the box that identifies it as the center

How to Use Center 3

This center can be located in a box anywhere in the classroom, home, or workplace. The box should be clearly marked as the conflict resolution box, and people must already know how to use the box before trying it with a real conflict. The parties involved can carry the box anywhere in the room or out of the room to use in solving a conflict.

Center 4: Pocket Folder

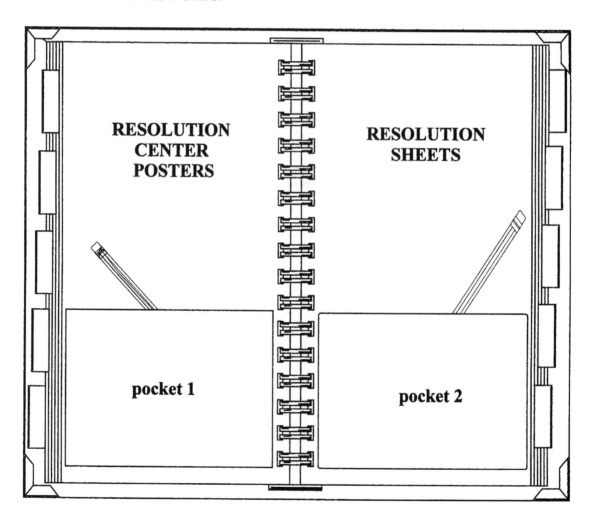

RESOLUTION
CENTER
POSTERS

RESOLUTION
SHEETS

pocket 1

pocket 2

Materials Needed:

- A pocket folder with or without a paper fastener in the middle
- Resolution sheets
- Posters stapled into a booklet for students to follow
- Two pencils to keep in one of the pockets of the folder

How to Use Center 4

In this center, you put posters in one pocket of the folder and the resolution sheets in the other pocket. On the front of the folder, you can post a cover sheet indicating that the folder is the conflict resolution center. This folder can travel anywhere in the room and can be used at desks, in hallways, and so on. We suggest that you have several conflict center folders available to students and that they be kept in a central location.

CONFLICT RESOLUTION BOOKLET

NAME_____

COVER SHEET

CONFLICT RESOLUTION AWARD

PRESENTED TO

_____

For successfully using thinking, writing,
reading, drawing, listening, and communication skills to solve problems
and resolve conflict!

Congratulations!

_____

Date: _____

CONGRATULATIONS! YOU ARE A PROBLEM SOLVER!

This award is presented to

_____

for using your thinking, reading, listening, writing, and communication skills to resolve conflict in a positive manner!

Using This Technique in Counseling

Settle Conflicts Right Now! is the perfect conflict resolution program for use in a counseling situation. Whether you are counseling children, adults, siblings, or spouses, this program will produce results. It supports the traditional school counselor's role as a facilitator for problem solving. Using this technique, the counselor's role as a facilitator is defined in the following way:

- You may ask clarifying questions but not impose a resolution.

- You may help the parties involved follow the procedure outlined in this chapter.

- You do not find fault, blame, or put yourself in the middle of the conflict by suggesting or dictating a resolution; only the parties involved can find the solution to their problem.

- You provide a safe environment with the materials needed for a resolution.

- You do not analyze why or what the parties involved did, but instead lead them through the process to resolve the conflict in a manner that is mutually satisfactory.

- You do teach the process of conflict resolution and the reasons why having compassion is better than giving pain.

Working With Groups in Counseling

Often counselors, particularly in the school setting, have to work with groups of individuals that have had fights, arguments, and hurt feelings. The process below is the procedure introduced in Chapters 1 and 3. In a counseling situation, this process is more comprehensive than the procedure used in the conflict resolution center. Individuals who need a facilitator present because of ongoing problems or unfamiliarity with the conflict center can see the counselor for help in resolving their problems.

The following steps use the hypothetical Person A and Person B to explain the process and how it is used in counseling. Of course, in reality you may have more than two people involved in a conflict.

Steps for Facilitating Conflict Resolution in a Counseling Setting

1. Tell the parties involved that there will be NO TALKING during the writing time unless they have a question pertaining to the resolution sheet they are using. Let them know that talking will be permitted during the exchange of needs or after the conflict resolution session is completed.

2. Use the counseling posters found at the end of this chapter to introduce information about conflict resolution to the students

3. Give each person copies of the conflict resolution forms found in Chapter 3 that match their appropriate age. For adults, this can be a simple piece of paper with lines on both sides. Have pens, pencils, clipboards, and markers available.

4. Tell each person to write down on Resolution Sheet 1 exactly what the other person did or said to them that they did not like. Each should use the other person's name on their worksheet when describing what happened and share their feelings about the action.

5. Check each person's worksheet to see if they are following the instructions given. If you, as the counselor, cannot understand something that is written, you can write a question on the worksheet asking for clarification. During this time, there is very little talking.

6. Have each person exchange worksheets. Tell them to silently read the other person's description of why they were upset. Direct each person to see if they can "discover the cause of the other person's pain." Tell them that while they are reading, they are not to judge, blame, condemn, or find fault with what the other person has written.

7. It does not matter whom you start with after Resolution Sheet 1 is completed. Ask Person B these questions:

- What doesn't Person A like?

- Why doesn't Person A like this?

- If the same things were to happen to you, would you feel the same pain that Person A did?

- Now do you understand Person A's pain?

Repeat the same questions with Person B.

8. Tell the people you are working with that now they have concrete evidence that trading pain does not work. It only increases the pain. People do not understand pain, but they do understand information. Trading information reduces pain or gets rid of pain or both.

9. Have everyone exchange worksheets so that each person has their original Resolution Sheet 1 back again.

10. Using Resolution Sheet 2, tell Persons A and B to list exactly what they think should be done to stop this conflict.

11. Provide ample writing time at this point. Check to see that everyone is following the instructions. The wants and/or needs of each student must be written very specifically and must be something that the other person can do without involving others in the solution. The wants and needs must also be related to the problem being solved. Direct each person to rewrite their needs if they are too vague or impossible to fulfill.

12. Exchange worksheets and have each person select a marker. Tell them to silently read what the other person wants them to do to resolve this conflict.

13. Tell Persons A and B that they must choose from each other's list what they will do to resolve the conflict. They are agreeing to items on the list not because they feel sorry for the other person, but because they understand the other person's pain, and they want to resolve the problem so that it will not occur again. Tell each person to look at the list of ideas that the other person has written. Direct each person to make a star, asterisk, initial, or their own symbol on the list next to the items they agree to do or stop doing for the other person.

14. Tell the parties involved that they will now have an opportunity to exchange information so that everyone will feel better. Ask Person A the following questions:

- What have you agreed to do to end this conflict?

- Do you have any questions to ask _____?

15. Repeat Step 14 for Person B. Have them shake hands when they have both stated what they will do to end the conflict.

16. Tell each person that they have now successfully resolved their conflict. Tell them that all they have to do now is exactly what they agreed to do on the other person's Resolution Sheet 2. Let them know that their word is their bond, and that the colored marks are their Color Code of Honor, showing that they will not go back on their promises. Finally, give each person a conflict resolution certificate. Make copies of the resolution sheets and give them to each person.

17. As a counselor, you will need to decide if copies of the resolution sheets will be kept on file for teachers, parents, and principals to see on a "need to know" basis.

Working With Individuals

It does not always take two or more people to create a conflict. Sometimes, individuals find conflict within themselves because of their environment, actions, or feelings. In a school, this individual can be the student who arrives at school angry and takes it out on his or her classmates. In the home, this can be the sibling or spouse who is having a bad day and whose mood reflects this attitude. Conflict within ourselves is often vented outward, with devastating effect on those around us. This kind of conflict creates depression, anger, and loss of control.

All individuals need to have a method for resolving personal conflict. The following is a method that can be modified for use in a variety of settings but is primarily for use in a school. In the school setting, children can find themselves in trouble because of their lack of self-control or poor social skills. Individual students sent to the counselor can use the I Have a Problem! worksheet that follows to help sort out their thinking and resolve their problem before returning to the classroom. The student is asked to first fill in the form without talking. Young children can draw pictures and older children can write. After the form is complete, each question on the form can be discussed with the student and the counseling posters can be used to reflect and explain the purpose of conflict resolution.

I Have a Problem!

(Processing of a Problem I Have at School)

Name_____ Date_____ Teacher_____

You have experienced what happens when you do not use the skill of *self-control* in the classroom. This experience has *taught* you something. This experience has provided you with *information*. Answer the questions below completely to help you to understand and use this information.

1. *What happens to me if I don't use self-control in the classroom?*

_____

_____

_____

_____

_____

2. *I need to do this to stop this problem:*

_____

_____

_____

_____

_____

3. *I don't want this to happen to me again! I want to have self-control! I plan to do the following to fix this problem and prevent it from happening again.*

   I will

   - _____

   - _____

   - _____

Counseling Posters

The counseling posters found on the following pages are designed to help the people you are working with understand the purpose of conflict resolution. We encourage the use of the posters before you begin the conflict resolution process. This will reduce the time needed for conflict resolution, and the persons you are working with will fully understand the purpose of this process.

LEARNING HOW TO SOLVE YOUR PROBLEMS WITH CONFLICT RESOLUTION!

COUNSELING POSTERS COVER SHEET

COUNSELING POSTER 1

COUNSELING POSTER 2

We know that when we have a conflict with other people, they hurt inside just like we do!

We are the SAME because we can all feel the SAME PAIN!

COUNSELING POSTER 3

Our bodies do not understand PAIN! We know our bodies are not meant to receive PAIN! We are meant to...

COUNSELING POSTER 4

. . .receive information from each other!
Trading information does not hurt!
Trading information ends the pain of conflict!

COUNSELING POSTER 5

INFORMATION!
This is what we understand!
We understand information
better than
verbal abuse
or
physical abuse!

COUNSELING POSTER 6

By trading information, we can heal each other's pain!

That is what conflict resolution is all about!

COUNSELING POSTER 7

COUNSELING POSTER 8

COUNSELING POSTER 9

6

Dealing With
Family Situations

Family conflicts are similar to conflicts found in schools. The goal of family conflict resolution is the facilitation of communication as well as the resolution of conflict. Consequently, the resolution of conflict in the family can be initiated by following the same type of program detailed in previous chapters. In the beginning, we recommend that the family meet to discuss the need for conflict resolution. The family must address the following key questions when establishing a conflict resolution program in the home:

- Who will use this program in your home—parents and children, or children only?

- Who will decide when to use the program? Will it be used with every conflict or just major problems that haven't been resolved through rules or choices?

- Where will the conflict resolution center be located in the house?

Answering these key questions will allow the family to identify their needs. This program can be used for everyone in the home. In addition to resolving sibling conflicts, it can be used very successfully between spouses and between parents and children. It is particularly useful with teenagers. This chapter will provide you with the procedures for using *Settle Conflicts Right Now!* in the home.

General Instructions for Home Use

The procedures for resolving conflict in the home are very similar to the procedures found in Chapter 3 for resolving school conflicts. Instructions for making a conflict resolution center can be found in Chapter 4. The following are the steps family members follow when using *Settle Conflicts Right Now!*

Step 1   The people involved in the conflict need to find a place at home where they can write and be comfortable. The kitchen table, dining room table, or bedroom are good locations. This place will be called the conflict resolution center.

Step 2   Each person writes on a regular piece of paper, or uses Resolution Sheet 1 from Chapter 3, to answer this question: What is the problem?

Step 3   Each person trades their paper and reads what the other person has written about the problem. At this time, each person can ask questions about what was written. The questions can be written on the other person's paper or asked orally.

Step 4   Papers are given back to their owners. If there are questions written on the paper, they should be answered now either orally or in writing. Papers are traded back and forth until all questions are answered.

Step 5   On the back of the paper or on Resolution Sheet 2, each person responds to this statement: What I need to solve this problem!

Step 6   Papers are again traded and read by each person. Each person makes a check mark or asterisk next to the items on the list that they agree to do for the other person to end the problem.

Step 7 Papers are given back to their owner. The checked areas on individual papers are the items the other person agrees to do. This becomes a personal contract to end the problem.

It is important to remember that conflict resolution requires compromise and that not all items will probably be checked on Resolution Sheet 2. The important thing is to end up with solutions to stop the fight.

Setting Up a Family Conflict Resolution Center

Setting up a family conflict resolution center is one way of helping your children resolve sibling conflicts, parent-child conflicts, and even parent-parent conflicts. This center can be placed anywhere in your home, but when deciding on the place, you might consider the following factors:

- The conflict center needs to be in a place where people can draw or write.
- The conflict center needs to be in a place where the materials can be permanently stored or can be easily transported to the location.
- The conflict center needs to be in a place or room that is comfortable for all people involved.

For the center to be most effective, children and parents must observe a few ground rules.

Ground Rules for Parents

- The children must be taught to use the center before it is actually used for conflict resolution in a real-life situation.
- The center should be used as soon as possible after the conflict occurs.
- The parents need to decide what conflicts are going to be handled with normal discipline and what conflicts will be resolved with the center. This must be clearly explained to the child.
- The parents must be prepared to use the center themselves by writing and resolving, just like the student, in good faith.
- The parents must honor the child's request if he or she asks to use the center.

Ground Rules for Children

- Children must use the center if requested by their parents.
- Children must be prepared to use the center by writing, drawing, and resolving in good faith.
- Children may request to use the center at any time.

Activity Cards

The following activity cards can be used as hypothetical situations for children to use to practice using the home conflict resolution center. You can make your own cards by writing down a sibling conflict situation from the past and having the children follow the Settle Conflicts Right Now! process to resolve the problem. They can then compare their original solution to the one created with the conflict center to see which works best.

ACTIVITY CARD 1

Home Situation

Jacob is 6 years old and his sister, Janice, is 8. They constantly fight over everything, especially when they are in the car. They fight over who sits next to the window. They fight over what music they will listen to on the tape player. They fight over each other's toys. Mom and Dad want peace when they are in the car and are tired of yelling and punishing both kids. What can be done to solve this problem?

ACTIVITY CARD 2

Home Situation

Jonathan usually has homework every night, but he frequently waits until he has been reminded by his mother to get working. She gets frustrated because she feels he is old enough to do his homework without being reminded. She is further frustrated by the fact that she has to remind him over and over every night to keep working and finish up. He hates doing homework and avoids getting started by waiting until he is reminded. He also hates being nagged to get his homework done. What can be done to solve this problem?

Activity Card 3

Home Situation

Susan's mom works an afternoon shift at a local business, so Susan goes home after school to an empty house. Susan knows that she is supposed to start on her homework when she gets home and her mother will be home by 6:30 p.m. every evening. Her dad works until 7:00 p.m. Susan is tired of going home and being alone, so she starts going downtown with her friends on the bus. She is careful to always be back before 6:30, but her homework isn't getting done. When her grades begin to fall, her parents start to wonder why. Eventually, the whole story is revealed when Susan's mom comes home early with a headache and finds that Susan is not home. She is very worried and calls all of Susan's friends. She discovers that Susan is downtown. When Susan returns home, she is surprised to find her mother at home. Susan's mom is shocked to discover that Susan hasn't been coming home, and she is angry, as well as relieved, that she is safe. They have angry words with each other. Susan is unhappy that her mother is working and that she can't go downtown with her friends. Her mother is unhappy that Susan deceived her. How can this conflict be resolved?

Resource A: Samples

The following samples illustrate how each type of conflict resolution sheet is used. Student examples involving real conflicts were *not* used in order to protect the words and identity of the students involved. Instead, the samples on the following pages are fictitious and were provided by 10-year-old Katie Osier. She was introduced to the technique using Activity Cards 1 and 2 in Chapter 3. The samples are to provide you with a visual representation of how the technique looks when students apply it. The following gives a brief background of each sample:

Sample 1 This sample illustrates how the drawing method for younger children is used to resolve conflict. Activity Card 1 from Chapter 3 was used to introduce the technique. The sample shows the students' perception of the conflict and resolution of the problem.

Sample 2 This sample illustrates how the writing method is used to resolve conflict. The conflict illustrated is from Activity Card 2 in Chapter 3.

DRAW THE PROBLEM!

Kateesha   Mariah

**RESOLUTION
SHEET
1**

NAME: _Character: Mariah_

NAME: Character: Kateesha

RESOLUTION SHEET 1

DRAW THE SOLUTION!

Walking away and leaving each other alone.

Kateesha

Mariah

RESOLUTION SHEET 2

NAME: Character: Kateesha

WHAT'S THE PROBLEM?

Directions: In the space below, describe what was said or done to you that you did not like!

Tell how you felt when this experience happened to you. Tell what you did!

NAME Character: Sam

I brought baseball cards to school without letting my parents know. My two friends said that James stole them, and when we got back to the classroom, he put them back. The cards are still in my backpack, but my friends want me to beat up James. James says that Keith and Kenya are lying. I don't believe him. Now we are in the office in trouble. James has been a bully since kindergarten. I think he took my cards and then put them back.

RESOLUTION SHEET 1

WHAT'S THE PROBLEM?

Directions: In the space below, describe what was said or done to you that you did not like!
Tell how you felt when this experience happened to you. Tell what you did!

NAME Character: James

I did not steal those dumb baseball cards. I have plenty of them. Keith and Kenya say that I stole them. I didn't even go to the classroom. Now Sam has challenged me to a fight. I don't want to beat him up. I would get in more trouble. Sam would believe anything from Kenya and Keith.

RESOLUTION SHEET 1

WHAT I NEED TO SOLVE THIS PROBLEM!

Directions: You have been hurt! You want something to happen that will help you feel better. Clearly describe what you think should happen to solve this problem!

NAME *Character: Sam*

1. I want James to confess that he stole my cards.

2. I just want him to leave my stuff alone. ☆ J.

3. I just want him to say he is sorry for touching my stuff.

4. I will leave my stuff at home from now on. ☆ J. S.

RESOLUTION SHEET 2

WHAT I NEED TO SOLVE THIS PROBLEM!

Directions: You have been hurt! You want something to happen that will help you feel better. Clearly describe what you think should happen to solve this problem!

NAME _Character: James_

1. I want Sam to not listen to Keith or Kenya.

2. I want Sam to leave his stuff at home. ☆ S.

3. I won't ever get into Sam's backpack. ☆ J. S.

4. I want Sam to check things out before he believes other people. ☆ S.

RESOLUTION SHEET 2

Resource B:
Frequently Asked Questions

This last section contains frequently asked questions and answers about this program.

1. *Who can use this program?* Anyone in need of conflict resolution age 5 and above can use this program. It was written primarily for teachers, students, parents, counselors, and school administrators.

2. *What is the idea behind this program?* The program is based on the idea that children and adults are problem solvers following a cycle of problem solving. This cycle is caused by the pain that we each suffer when we have a problem. The cycle is one of identifying the problem, gathering information, sharing information, evaluating consequences, identifying needs, and creating a solution. Solutions are based on individuals' identifying their needs and sharing that information with others.

3. *How is this idea applied in the program?* The program teaches a technique that can be applied through drawing or writing. Each component asks three questions:

- What is the problem?
- What do I think needs to be done to solve the problem?
- What am I willing to do to end this problem?

4. *What are the main components of the program?* This book comes with a program for managing conflict with individuals in Grades K-6. It has materials for teaching the program at school and home as well as information for creating a conflict resolution center.

5. *What skills are involved in using this program?* The program reinforces the basic cognitive skills taught in school: reading, writing, thinking, listening, sharing, and communication.

6. *How long does this program take to learn?* The program can be taught to individuals so they can use it independently in 15 to 30 minutes. Before using the program with real-life conflict, it is useful to hold three or four practice sessions.

7. *How long does this program take to use?* It takes an average of 15 to 30 minutes to resolve a problem using this method.

8. *What happens if this method doesn't end the problem forever?* In our 10 years of working with this program, we have not had individuals initiate the same conflict over again after using this method. We feel this is because our method allows all parties involved to feel justice and have their ideas heard without condemnation and judgment. Practice does make perfect; there may be a time when children need more practice repeating the process.

9. *How can children use this program by themselves? Don't they need a mediator?* Most people, including children, do not have a mediator readily available to help them solve conflicts when they occur in life. Our approach allows individuals to use their own resources to solve their problems. The program provides a framework for resolving conflict. Individuals are taught how to use this framework and to apply it to conflict situations. A conflict resolution center is available so that other people do not have to get involved.

10. *Can this program be used with large groups of children who are in conflict?* Yes, but you may have to adapt the program to meet their individual needs. The program is flexible and designed to be adapted. With a large group (six or more), you may want the group to dictate their responses to you. Chapter 5 shows how a facilitator can work with this process.

11. *What if an individual is so angry that they refuse to write or cooperate?* Several things can be done with this individual. You might use the drawing resolution sheets instead of the writing sheets. You might have the individual do Resolution Sheet 1 the first day and Resolution Sheet 2 the second day when they have calmed down.

You might put the individual in time-out until they are ready to solve the problem. You might have the counselor facilitate a solution. You might suggest that this program is one option for the individual. The second option might be regular disciplinary measures that match the conflict.

12. *Would you use this method with every little problem that individuals have with each other?* When you use this program will depend on the severity of the conflict, how long the conflict has been going on, and the willingness of the parties involved to resolve their problem. We find that individuals internalize this approach and use it before the conflict becomes a problem that needs resolution. The ultimate aim of the program is for individuals to evaluate their needs and choose good solutions for their problems.

13. *What makes this book different from other conflict resolution books?* We feel that the following points identify the areas that make our book unique:

- Practical, fast, effective, easy-to-follow chapters and directions

- No mediator necessary for individuals to resolve problems

- Can be used by children and adults

- Can be used in school and home settings

- Allows individuals to use higher-level thinking and problem-solving skills

- Reinforces thinking, reading, writing, listening, and communications skills

- Uses a comprehensive one-book program that is reproducible

- Empowers individuals to SOLVE THEIR OWN PROBLEMS!

CORWIN
PRESS

The Corwin Press logo—a raven striding across an open book—represents the happy union of courage and learning. We are a professional-level publisher of books and journals for K–12 educators, and we are committed to creating and providing resources that embody these qualities. Corwin's motto is "Success for All Learners."